I Want To Cry But I Don't Know Why

EILEEN BELLINI

(ILLUSTRATED BY SINCLAIR JACKSON)

Dedication

To sweet George who inspired this book and to Genevieve who is the best big sister a boy could have! I love you both so much!

"I want to cry but I don't know why,"
said little George.

"Did you run and fall?

Did you scrape your knee?

"Noooo," cried the boy.
"It's not like that, you see.
I just feel like crying, so please let me be!"

Sister Genevieve popped by
and wanted to know

"Did you lose your big stick?

Did your hand get stuck in the cookie jar?"

"Noooo!" cried George with tears in his eyes. "I just want to cry and I don't know why!"

Then dad jumped in
and asked with a sigh,

Were you eating a snack
and to your surprise,

"Nooooo!" said little George,
with a trace of a smile,
"That's so silly, dad.
I just need to be for a while."

So mom, dad, and sis sat still
with nothing to say.

Then Mom gave George a tickle...
and his tears went away

They hugged and kissed his
sweet little head, and he grinned and
giggled and finally said.

I don't want to cry
and I think I know why!

He hugged them back and shouted with glee, "I'm feeling much better because you love me."

The End

Acknowledgments

Many thanks to Gary Woonteller for his skillful edits and of course Sinclair, their maternal grandma, for her inspirational illustrations. It was a labor of love.